OMNIVORES AND HERBIVORES

Michael Leach
and Meriel Lland

Enslow Publishing
101 W. 23rd Street
Suite 240
New York, NY 10011

enslow.com

This edition published in 2020 by Enslow Publishing, LLC
101 W. 23rd Street, Suite 240, New York, NY 10011

Cataloging-in-Publication Data

Names: Leach, Michael. | Lland, Meriel.
Title: Omnivores and herbivores / Michael Leach and Meriel Lland.
Description: New York : Enslow Publishing, 2020. | Series: Animal explorers | Includes bibliographical references
and index.
Identifiers: ISBN 9781978509917 (library bound) | ISBN 9781978509894 (pbk.) | ISBN 9781978509900 (6 pack)
Subjects: LCSH: Omnivores—Juvenile literature. | Herbivores—Juvenile literature.
Classification: LCC QL756.5 L43 2020 | DDC591.5'3—dc23

Printed in the United States of America

To Our Readers: We have done our best to make sure all website addresses in this book were active and appropriate
when we went to press. However, the author and the publisher have no control over and assume no liability for the
material available on those websites or on any websites they may link to. Any comments or suggestions can be sent by
email to customerservice@enslow.com.

Photo Credits:
Every attempt has been made to clear copyright. Should there be any inadvertent omission,
please apply to the publisher for rectification.
Key: b-bottom, t-top, c-center, l-left, r-right

Alamy: 4–5 (Ian Cruickshank), 11t (Egmont Strigl), 20–21 (Suzi Eszterhas/Minden Pictures); FLPA: 10–11 (ZSSD/Minden
Pictures), 12–13 (Erica Olsen), 16–17 (Frans Lanting), 16cl (Juergen & Christine Sohns/Minden Pictures), 22cr (Terry
Whittaker); Shutterstock: cover and title page; 4cl (Puwadol Jaturawutthichai), 4br (Alen thien), 5tr (Giedrilius), 5cl
(David Bokuchava), 5br (Dennis van de Water), 6–7 (Delbars), 6br (Spreadthesign), 7tl & 31br (Bildagentur Zoona
GmbH), 7b (jdross75), 8–9 (Nuamfolio), 8tr (Utopia_88), 9tr (Maquiladora), 9cr (Nivlac921), 10tr (Emma Geary), 10br
(Spreadthesign), 13tl (T Wilbertz), 13c (MarciSchauer), 13br (Spreadthesign), 14–15 (Aleksey Sagitov), 14c (Nesrudheen
Pariyarath), 14br (Spreadthesign), 15tr (Sergey Didenko), 16br (Noahsu), 17br (Yana Kazuar), 18–19 (Natalia Paklina),
18cr (Khai9000Pictures), 18bl (Arto Hakola), 19br (Yana Kazuar), 20c & 31bl (Andril Slonchak), 20br (Creative Mood),
21cr 32br (Jason Benz Bennee), 22–23 (aapsky), 22cl (Jearu), 22br (Spreadthesign), 24–25 (Rudmer Zwerver), 24cr
(michael sheehan), 24br (Rhoeo), 25b (Vladimir Wrangel), 26tr (Ondrej Prosicky), 26tl (Bigone), 26cr (RPBaiao), 26bl
(BlueOrange Studio), 26br (meunierd), 27tl (Yusnizam Yusof), 27tr (rorue), 27cl (Brian Lasenby), 27br (colin robert
vamdell), 27bl (Neil Burton), 28c (Four Oaks), 29tr (Roop_Dey), 29br (Pascale Gueret).

CONTENTS

Introduction

An animal is a living organism made up of cells. It feeds, senses, and responds to its surroundings, moves, and reproduces. Scientists have identified nearly nine million species of living animals, but there are many more to be found.

Rhinoceros hornbills are birds that live in Southeast Asian rain forests. Birds are warm–blooded animals with backbones. They have wings and most can fly.

Life Appears

Single-celled life forms appeared around four billion years ago. Sponges—the first animals—appeared a billion years ago. Over time, more complicated animals evolved and some also became extinct. Dinosaurs were the dominant land animals for 165 million years before they died out 65 million years ago.

Fossilized skull of the dinosaur *Tyrannosaurus rex*

Leaf beetle, an insect

Classifying Life

Scientists organize living things into groups with shared characteristics. The two main kinds of animal are ones with backbones (vertebrates) and ones without (invertebrates). Arthropods make up the biggest invertebrate group. They have segmented bodies and jointed limbs. Insects, spiders, and crabs are all arthropods.

Warm- and Cold-Blooded

Most animals are ectothermic, or "cold-blooded." Their body temperature is controlled by their environment. Mammals and birds are endothermic, or "warm-blooded." Their bodies can generate their own heat, so they can survive in much colder habitats.

Musk ox, a mammal

Langurs in a city

Fragile Earth

We are lucky to share our world with an extraordinary richness of animals. It is important to protect our wildlife. When humans pollute or damage the environment, we harm both animals and people. The future is in our hands.

Giant leaf–tailed gecko, vulnerable because of habitat loss

Animal Habitats

The place where an animal lives is called its habitat. Animals have evolved to inhabit just about every environment on Earth, from tropical rain forests and coral reefs to deserts, mountaintops, and ice floes. They even survive in cities.

Omnivores and Herbivores

Some mammals eat both meat and plants. These are the omnivores, adaptable species that survive on a wide variety of food. Herbivores are specialists that eat only vegetation— leaves, grass, flowers, bark, and other plant parts.

PLAINS ZEBRA

EQUUS QUAGGA

Habitat: Forests, grasslands, scrub; East and Southern Africa
Length: Male 7.5 feet (2.3 m); female 6.6 feet (2 m)
Weight: Male 661 pounds (300 kg); female 551 pounds (250 kg)
Diet: Grass, low-growing plants
Life span: Up to 25 years
Wild population: 750,000; Near Threatened

Varied Diet

Omnivores have more choice than specialists. They can eat foods that are in season and change their diet if a particular food source dries up.

Zebra and wildebeest are herbivores. Grazers have sharp front teeth called incisors to snip off plants, and big, flat back teeth called molars for chewing.

A Eurasian badger feasts on fruit when it is in season, eats worms when it's raining, and catches small mammals when it can.

Digestive Challenges

Plants are hard to digest. Some animals, such as rabbits, get around this by eating their droppings. As the food passes through the body a second time, they absorb any remaining goodness. Other animals simply take a long time to process their food.

Food passes through the human body in about 30 hours, but in a sloth this can take up to three weeks!

Elephants

Elephants evolved 50 million years ago. The two kinds alive today are African and Asian elephants. They live in family groups of up to 12 females and their calves, led by an older female called the matriarch. Adult male elephants live alone or in male-only herds.

African or Asian?

The African elephant is the world's largest land animal. One male weighed 24,000 pounds (11,000 kg). Asian elephants are smaller and have smaller ears. Their backs are flat or humped; the African elephant's back has a dip in the middle.

Elephant babies take longer to develop inside their mother than any other land mammal. The mother elephant is pregnant for 22 months.

The front teeth, or tusks, dig up roots and strip bark from trees. Inside the mouth, four huge molars grind up plant food.

The ears are used as fans to cool the elephant on hot days. Each elephant can be identified by the shape and size of its ears.

ASIAN ELEPHANT

ELEPHAS MAXIMUS
"LARGEST OX"

Habitat: Forests, scrub; South Asia
Length: Male 9.8 feet (3 m);
    female 8.9 feet (2.7 m)
Weight: Male 9,920 pounds (4,500 kg);
    female 6,063 pounds (2,750 kg)
Diet: Leaves, twigs, bark
Life span: Up to 60 years
Wild population: 40,000; Endangered

Trunk Talk

The elephant's trunk is an extension of its nose and top lip. It is incredibly sensitive and versatile. It can carry food and water into the mouth, squirt water, or spray dust. It is also used to touch and stroke.

Elephants suck up dust and then blow it over their back and shoulders. It acts as a sunscreen and keeps away insects.

The tail is 4 feet (1.3 m) long and tipped with long, thick hair. It can be flicked like a flyswatter to drive away insects.

The trunk is so complicated that it takes a calf a year to master using it! It can grasp, suck, touch, and smell.

Rhinos

The rhinoceros is the second-largest land animal after the elephant. It has a sturdy body, tough skin, and one or two defensive horns. There are five species. The white rhino and black rhino both live in Africa. The Indian, Javan, and Sumatran rhinos live in Asia.

The black rhino lives in dry grasslands in eastern Africa. It feeds on twigs, shoots, and leaves.

Rhino Communications

Scent is very important for rhinos. The largest part of their brain is devoted to processing it, and they mark their territory with dung and urine. Rhinos also use sound to communicate. They make an assortment of noises including squeals, snorts, growls, and moos.

Its extremely thick, hairless skin means the rhino overheats easily. Wallowing in mud is a good way to cool down, and the dried mud helps to stop sunburn.

WHITE RHINOCEROS

CERATOTHERIUM SIMUM

"HORNED BEAST WITH A FLAT NOSE"

Habitat: Grasslands; East and Southern Africa
Length: Male 13 feet (4 m); female 11.8 feet (3.6 m)
Weight: Male 5,512 pounds (2,500 kg); female 4,409 pounds (2,000 kg)
Diet: Grass, low-growing plants
Life span: Up to 50 years
Wild population: 20,000; Vulnerable

Rhinos in Danger

All five rhino species are under threat. Some people believe that powdered rhinoceros horn cures diseases. This isn't true, but the belief fuels an illegal trade of rhino horn and causes the slaughter of many animals.

Large, cup-shaped ears can swivel to pick up sounds from all around. Rhinos can even detect sounds when they are asleep.

Conservationists deliberately removed this Indian bull rhino's horn. They hope this will stop him being targeted by poachers.

Rhinoceros means "nose horn." The horn is made of keratin, the same substance that makes our hair and nails.

Rhinos have small eyes and poor eyesight. They only see well at close range. Anything more than 33 feet (10 m) away is out of focus.

11

Giraffes

The giraffe is the world's tallest animal, standing up to 18.7 feet (5.7 m) high. This hoofed mammal lives in female family groups on the African savannah, feeding on twigs and leaves from the treetops. There are nine subspecies, which are distinguished by the patterns of their coats.

Large eyes and great height give the giraffe excellent vision.

Both male and female giraffes have short horns covered in bristly hairs. The males butt these when they spar for dominance.

Like our fingerprints, no two giraffes have exactly the same markings.

Standing Tall

Giraffe calves can stand and walk within an hour of being born. They spend their lives standing up, and even sleep on their feet. Giraffes gallop at up to 30 miles (48 km) per hour and usually look graceful—unless they are drinking. Their legs are shorter than their necks, so they bend down very awkwardly!

A drinking giraffe is very vulnerable. It takes a while to stand back up straight again.

The giraffe can use its 18-inch- (46 cm) long tongue to grip a plant while its teeth strip off the leaves.

Zebra or Giraffe?

The okapi is a close cousin of the giraffe but it lacks the long neck and has stripes like a zebra. Hunted for its unusual and beautiful skin, as well as for meat, the okapi is endangered today. Its forest home is also threatened by illegal mining and logging.

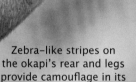

Zebra–like stripes on the okapi's rear and legs provide camouflage in its rain forest habitat.

GIRAFFE

GIRAFFA CAMELOPARDALIS "FAST-WALKING CAMEL LEOPARD"

Habitat: Savannah, forests; East and Southern Africa
Length: Male 18 feet (5.5 m); female 15.7 feet (4.8 m)
Weight: Male 2,646 pounds (1,200 kg); female 1,830 pounds (830 kg)
Diet: Leaves, twigs, bark
Life span: Up to 25 years
Wild population: Unknown; Vulnerable

Camels

There are two camel species: the one-humped dromedary and the two-humped Bactrian. Both types have been domesticated—used by humans for transportation and as a source of milk, meat, wool, and leather. There are no wild dromedaries today, but the remaining wild Bactrians live in Central Asia.

Ships of the Desert

Camels are suited to hot, dry environments. They can survive without water for months. They do not overheat, and are able to walk as far as 19 miles (30 km) in a day. At night, when the temperature in the desert drops, their shaggy hair keeps them warm.

Also known as the Arabian camel, the dromedary lives across the Middle East and North Africa.

WILD BACTRIAN CAMEL

CAMELUS FERUS

Habitat: Deserts, dry plains; Mongolia, China
Length: Male 9.8 feet (3 m);
   female 8.5 feet (2.6 m)
Weight: Male 1,653 pounds (750 kg);
   female 1,378 pounds (625 kg)
Diet: Plants
Life span: Up to 40 years
Wild population: 1,000; Critically Endangered

Camels' Cousins

Four members of the camel family live in South America. They are sure-footed but do not have humps. Guanacos and vicunas live wild in deserts and highlands. Llamas and alpacas have been domesticated as pack animals and to provide milk, meat, and soft, fleecy wool.

The guanaco is a survivor. Its body can cope in the dry Atacama Desert and at altitudes higher than 13,125 feet (4,000 m).

Long hairs inside the ears keep out sand but still let the camel hear.

Nostrils can close in dust storms. The camel can open them to breathe.

The camel's hump stores fat, not water. This fat can be broken down to provide energy when needed.

Each foot has two hooved toes that spread the weight and stop the camel from sinking into the sand.

Apes

Apes are primates that do not have tails. There are two groups. The great apes are humans, Central Africa's chimpanzees and gorillas, and the orangutan of Borneo and Sumatra. The lesser apes are the 18 gibbon species, which are smaller than their great ape cousins.

The orangutan is the only ape that lives alone instead of in groups. However, a young orangutan stays with its mother for the first eight years of life.

Intelligent Beasts

The great apes are large, intelligent animals. They have very advanced brains, great memories, and are good at solving problems. Chimpanzees are the most frequent tool users. They use sticks as "fishing rods" to collect termites from termite mounds. They also shape sticks into "spears" for hunting small primates. Chimps are the only apes that regularly eat meat. The protein helps to fuel their big brains.

A chimpanzee slurps up termites from its "fishing" stick. It even frays the end of the stick so it will pick up more insects.

Under Threat

All the non-human great apes are endangered, and gorillas and orangutans are critically endangered. They have been affected by habitat destruction, hunting, and disease, and have also been removed from the wild for the illegal pet trade.

Today the mountain gorilla's range is limited to the Virunga Mountains and one national park in Uganda.

An orangutan's face is bare, though males have fleshy cheek pads. The rest of the body is covered in straggly orange hair.

Sensitive lips test fruits for ripeness. The orangutan also makes lip-smacking sounds to communicate.

BORNEAN ORANGUTAN

PONGO PYGMAEUS
"LITTLE PERSON OF THE FOREST"

Habitat: Rain forests; Borneo
Length: Male 4.6 feet (1.4 m); female 4 feet (1.2 m)
Weight: Male 187 pounds (85 kg); female 82 pounds (37 kg)
Diet: Fruit, shoots, leaves
Life span: Up to 45 years
Wild population: 55,000; Critically Endangered

Monkeys and Lemurs

Monkeys and prosimians (lemurs, lorises, and bushbabies) are primates, like the apes, so they climb well and have opposable thumbs that can pick up objects. They can be distinguished from the apes because they usually have tails. They also have smaller bodies and smaller brains.

Monkey Business

There are around 260 monkey species. The "New World" monkeys that live in the treetops of Central and South American forests have prehensile (gripping) tails. They include tamarins, squirrel monkeys, and marmosets. "Old World" monkeys live in Africa and Asia in forests, grasslands, scrubland, swamps, and even cities. They include baboons, macaques, and langurs.

A spectacled langur baby is born with orange fur. It turns dusky brown by the age of six months.

Madagascar's Stars

Lemurs live only on the island of Madagascar. There are more than 100 species, ranging from Madame Berthe's mouse lemur—the smallest primate at just 1.1 ounces (30 g)—to the indri at 21 pounds (9.5 kg). More than 90 percent of lemur species are under threat of extinction.

The endangered ring-tailed lemur lives in dry forests and bush in Madagascar.

The male mandrill is the largest monkey. It can be almost 3.3 feet (1 m) long and weigh up to 79 pounds (36 kg). Mandrills live in rain forests and grassland in West Africa.

Mandrills communicate with scent, calls, and visual signs. This threat yawn shows off the male's sharp canines.

MANDRILL
MANDRILLUS SPHINX

Habitat: Forests, farmland, grasslands; West Africa
Length: Male 35.4 inches (90 cm);
  female 27.6 inches (70 cm)
Weight: Male 70.5 pounds (32 kg);
  female 57.3 pounds (26 kg)
Diet: Leaves, fruit, insects, small mammals
Life span: Up to 20 years
Wild population: Unknown; Vulnerable

Marsupials

Kangaroos, koalas, and their relatives are marsupials, or pouched mammals. Most mammal babies develop inside their mother's body, and many can walk or even run shortly after birth. Marsupial babies are born tiny, underdeveloped, and helpless. They crawl into their mother's pouch to carry on growing there.

Australian Life

There are a few marsupial species, such as the opossums, in North and South America. However, most live in Australia and New Guinea. They include kangaroos, koalas, wombats, wallabies, quokkas, and Tasmanian devils. Pouched mammals were the only kind of mammal in Australia until early settlers brought non-native dogs, mice, and rabbits.

The large nose sniffs out fresh eucalyptus leaves and scent markings left by other koalas.

The red kangaroo is the largest marsupial. This young male will grow almost as tall as a human, be able to leap 29.5 feet (9 m), and run at 44 miles (70 km) per hour.

The mother's pouch holds the baby koala, which is called a joey.

KOALA

PHASCOLARCTOS CINEREUS "ASHY POUCHED BEAR"

Habitat: Forests, scrub; Eastern Australia
Length: Male 30 inches (75 cm); female 28 inches (70 cm)
Weight: Male 19.8 pounds (9 kg); female 15.4 pounds (7 kg)
Diet: Eucalyptus leaves
Life span: Up to 20 years
Wild population: 75,000; Vulnerable

All Sorts of Diet

Kangaroos and wallabies eat any grass or leaves, while koalas feed mainly on eucalyptus. Insect-eating marsupials, such as bilbies, bandicoots, and numbats, have pointed snouts for drawing minibeasts out of bark or soil. The Tasmanian devil is the largest carnivorous marsupial.

The Tasmanian devil is the size of a small dog but it can take prey as large as a medium kangaroo.

Extremely thick, waterproof fur protects the koala against hot and cold temperatures.

Rodents

Found everywhere except Antarctica, rodents make up 40 percent of all mammals. There are around 1,500 species, including mice, rats, squirrels, beavers, and porcupines. Capybaras are the largest rodents. Guinea pigs, gerbils, and hamsters are all rodents too.

Like all rodents, the red squirrel has teeth that never stop growing. It sometimes gnaws on old deer antlers to get extra calcium for its teeth.

Food and Family

Rodents have sharp incisor teeth that keep growing throughout their lives. They can eat very hard food without their teeth wearing down. Some species eat and spoil human food and spread disease. Brown rats, black rats, and house mice are all pests. Rodents can live solitary lives, like the dormouse, or stay in family groups, like the beaver. Ground squirrels and mole rats form huge colonies.

The black-tailed prairie dog is a kind of ground squirrel. One colony in Texas contained an estimated 400 million prairie dogs and covered an area of 25,000 square miles (64,000 sq km).

Ready for Anything!

Rodents live in a variety of habitats. Lemmings survive average winter temperatures of –30°F (–34°C) in the Arctic tundra. Kangaroo rats and gerbils have adapted to life in the desert environments.

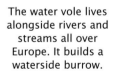

The water vole lives alongside rivers and streams all over Europe. It builds a waterside burrow.

EUROPEAN RED SQUIRREL

SCIURUS VULGARIS
"COMMON SQUIRREL"

Habitat: Forests; Europe, Asia
Length: 15 inches (38 cm)
Weight: 1.3 pounds (600 g)
Diet: Seeds, nuts, fungi, berries
Life span: Up to 20 years
Wild population: Unknown; Vulnerable

The red squirrel has a great sense of smell. This helps it to sniff out the stores of nuts that it buries to survive the winter.

The bushy tail provides balance as the squirrel leaps from branch to branch. Flicking and waving the tail is also a way to communicate.

The busy front paws collect pine cones, hazelnuts, beechnuts, and berries. Squirrels also eat buds, fungi, birds' eggs, and sap.

Paler fur on the squirrel's belly blurs the outline of its body, and makes it more difficult for predators to see.

Wild Pigs

Wild pigs are intelligent and adaptable hoofed mammals native to Europe, Africa, and Asia, and introduced to Australia and the Americas. They include wild boar, peccaries, warthogs, and bush pigs. Wild pigs have stocky bodies, short legs, and long snouts with large nostrils.

Wild Pig Diet

Pigs are omnivores. They forage for roots, bulbs, nuts, berries, and seeds. They also eat worms, beetle grubs, birds' eggs, small mammals, reptiles, and amphibians. The warthog is the only wild pig that eats grass. It lives on the African savannah.

Pigs have a good sense of smell that can detect food buried underground. They use their snouts to dig, touch, and feel.

Wild boar piglets have striped coats that help them to blend in with the leaf litter. The stripes start to fade at about three months.

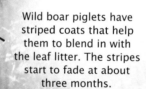

The warthog is named for the warty lumps on its head. Its long upper teeth, or tusks, can grow 12 inches (30 cm) long.

WILD BOAR

SUS SCROFA "DIGGING PIG"

Habitat: Forests, farmland, grasslands; Europe, Asia, North Africa
Length: Male 5.6 feet (1.7 m); female 4.3 feet (1.3 m)
Weight: Male 419 pounds (190 kg); female 298 pounds (135 kg)
Diet: Plants, insects, eggs, small animals
Life span: Up to 14 years
Wild population: Unknown; Least Concern

Wild boars live in groups called sounders, made up of sows and their piglets. Sounders usually contain about 20 animals.

Pigs are short-sighted. They cannot see detail from a distance but they are good at spotting movement.

Terrific Tusks

Male wild pigs have enlarged canine teeth called tusks that continue growing throughout their life. The babirusa's upward-curving tusks pierce through its snout and will eventually cut into its skull if it does not wear them down regularly.

The babirusa lives near rivers in Indonesian rain forests. Only the male has the huge, curved tusks.

Fun Facts

Now that you have discovered lots about omnivores and herbivores, boost your knowledge further with these 10 quick facts!

Hippos eat up to 77 pounds (35 kg) of grass a day—but these "herbivores" will also kill and eat impalas (antelopes).

An elephant's trunk has more than 40,000 muscles. The whole human body contains fewer than 1,000 muscles!

Rhinos move fast in spite of their bulk. Black and Indian rhinos are the speediest—they can charge at 34 miles (55 km) per hour.

Giraffes and humans have the same number of bones in their neck—seven. Each giraffe vertebra can be 10 inches (25 cm) long.

An angry or fearful camel can bring up its stomach contents to spit at its enemy. The partly digested food has a terrible smell.

Orangutans' powerful arms are one-and-a-half times longer than their legs. A male's arm span can be 7 feet (2 m) from fingertip to fingertip.

The Barbary macaque is the only macaque species found outside Asia. It is also the only wild primate that lives in Europe.

The female Virginia opossum has the shortest pregnancy of any mammal—just 12 days.

Brown rats are the world's most common wild mammal. In Paris, France, there are four rats for every person.

There are around one billion domestic pigs around the world today. They are all descended from the wild boar.

Your Questions Answered

We know an incredible amount about the creatures that populate our planet—from the deepest oceans to the highest mountains. But there is always more to discover. Scientists are continuing to find out incredible details about the lives of apes, rodents, and other mammals that hunt and forage for their food. Here are some questions about plant-eating and omnivorous mammals that can help you discover more about these fascinating creatures.

In an elephant herd, larger animals shield smaller, younger ones.

Why are elephants so big?

Today's elephants are the largest land animals, but they evolved from creatures that were about the size of a mouse! Over more than 24 million generations, they gradually evolved into larger and larger animals. Their size and weight are a form of protection—predators only stand a chance if they manage to attack a very young member of an elephant family. Which is why most elephant families travel in formations whereby the largest, heaviest members shield the smaller, more vulnerable animals.

Do the markings on a giraffe serve a purpose?

As with many animals, the giraffe's spots act as a form of camouflage, helping the animal blend in with its surroundings. But they also serve another purpose. Each spot has an intricate system of blood vessels underneath it that helps the giraffe regulate its body temperature. If the giraffe is too hot, the vessels will allow more blood to flow through, and thereby help the body expel heat.

How closely are humans related to other big apes?

Through studies of anatomy and genetics, scientists have discovered that we are most closely related to chimpanzees. But the reason why we are related to other apes in the first place is that we all have a common ancestor—a type of creature that lived many thousands of years ago, and from which all of today's apes gradually developed. And that includes humans.

Chimpanzees often display human-like behavior.

Is the koala a bear?

Many people refer to them as "koala bears," because koalas have the appearance of a small bear. But although koalas and bears are both mammals, there is one key difference between them. While in bears, the young reach a stage of development inside their mothers that means they are able to move and engage with their surroundings when they are born, koala young are different. As they are marsupials, they are born at a very early, immature stage of development and carry on growing in their mother's pouch, until they are ready to move about independently. So the correct name is "koala," not "koala bear."

What makes an animal intelligent?

It is generally accepted that humans are the most intelligent animals on Earth, but how do other creatures compare? When establishing the intelligence of an animal, scientists look at various skills, all of which require complex thinking and reacting skills. These include being able to learn, reason, and solve problems, being self-aware and aware of the presence and feelings of those around them, the use of tools, creativity, use of language, and the ability to deceive.

Crows are rated as a particularly intelligent animal due to their use of tools and their ability to deceive.

Glossary

ape A large primate that doesn't have a tail, including humans, gorillas, and chimpanzees.

bull A large male animal.

camouflage To blend in with one's surroundings.

conservationist A person who works to protect wildlife and the environment.

defensive Used to protect oneself or someone/something.

deliberately On purpose.

domesticate To keep an animal as a pet.

dominance The power one holds over others.

extinct Describes an animal that has died out forever.

forage To search for food.

habitat An animal's natural environment.

herbivore An animal that eats plants.

keratin A protein that hair, feathers, hooves, horns, and other body features are made from.

mammal A warm-blooded vertebrate that has hair or fur and feeds its young on mother's milk.

marsupial A mammal that gives birth to underdeveloped young that carry on growing in a pouch on their mother's belly.

matriarch The female head of a family or clan; an elephant matriarch is the oldest female and leader of a family group.

monkey A primate that has a tail, including baboons, macaques, and marmosets.

omnivore An animal that eats plants and meat.

opposable thumb A thumb that can be placed opposite the fingers of the same hand to pick up or hold objects. All primates have this.

protein A nutrient that is needed for growth and repair.

rodent A mammal that has strong front teeth that never stop growing. Rodents gnaw to keep these teeth sharp and at the right length.

spar To fight without physically harming one's opponent.

tusk A long, pointed tooth or object that protrudes from the head of an animal.

Further Information

BOOKS

Davey, Owen. *Mad About Monkeys*. London, UK: Flying Eye Books, 2015.

Riggs, Kate. *Elephants*. Mankato, MN: The Creative Company, 2013.

Savage, Stephen. *Focus on Mammals*. New York, NY: Gareth Stevens Publishing, 2012.

Spelman, Lucy. *Animal Encyclopedia: 2,500 Animals with Photos, Maps, and More!* Washington, DC: National Geographic Kids, 2012.

Spilsbury, Louise, and Mike Gordon. *What is Evolution*? London, UK: Wayland Books, 2016.

WEBSITES

DK Find Out!: Inside a Mammal
www.dkfindout.com/us/animals-and-nature/mammals/inside-mammal/
Find out all about the skeletons of mammals. You can also take a quiz.

Ducksters: Mammals
www.ducksters.com/animals/mammals.php
Head to this website to find out all there is to know about mammals.

Index